Designing with Natural Forms

Designing with Natural Forms

Natalie d'Arbeloff
Photography by Ted Sebley

Watson-Guptill Publications/New York

Acknowledgments

I wish to thank Ian Simpson, Head of Coordinated Studies and members of the staff of the Visual Research Department of Hornsey College of Art, London, who took the time and trouble to show me and talk about their students' work. I am especially grateful to Mrs Joanna Shelton in this respect, and to all the students she introduced me to, and I regret that there has not been more space in this book to include as many examples of their work as I would have liked.

London 1972   N.d'A.

First published in the United States of America 1973 by Watson-Guptill Publications, One Astor Plaza, New York, N.Y. 10036, U.S.A.

Manufactured in Great Britain
First printing, 1973
Reprinted 1974

Contents

There is a spirit hidden in things which says: order, structure;
there is a spirit hidden in things which says: play, variety. You
have only to look at a flower, a tree, a man, to know that these
two forces do not combat each other nor are they in the least
contradictory. In their conjunction, it is these forces which
compose, on the basis of a simple, always renewed geometric
theme, the diverse styles of the world we live in, the immense
modulation of the universe.

Michel Seuphor
Translated from: *Le Style et Le Cri*,
Editions du Seuil, Paris 1965

Getting to the bottom of things: what does this mean? First of
all, things move. To get to the bottom of them or perceive their
meaning, one would have to go to the bottom of movement
itself. But I am *within* movement, I myself am movement. How,
then, shall I know it? . . . Adapt, adapt! This is the pass-word.
Bend with the movement of the wave. And sing a little.

Michel Seuphor
Translated from: *Le Don de la Parole*,
Librairie-Editions Mallier, Paris 1970

The essence of discovery is that unlikely marriage of cabbages
and kings—of previously unrelated frames of reference or
universes of discourse—whose union will solve the previously
insoluble problem.

Arthur Koestler
The Act of Creation,
Hutchinson & Co., London 1964

Let us learn always to receive further surprises.

Ivan Illich
Celebration of Awareness,
Calder & Boyars, London 1971

Introduction

An art student once said to me: 'I don't know what to do with what I see.' This is a book of ideas which attempt to answer that question. I am suggesting that the 'what' and 'how' to do come out of the process of seeing itself, providing it is a kind of seeing which is a persistent focusing of the whole attention on only one subject for an extended period of time. Such 'seeing' does not necessarily come naturally. It has to be developed and constantly practised; and it is not the exclusive priority of the visual artist. I hope that anyone concerned with observation and creative expression will be able to use this book, adapting it to their own requirements.

It is generally assumed that concentrating means shutting out everything but the subject one is trying to grasp, in an intense and often painful effort of attention. I ask the reader to accompany me on my exploration of a different approach to concentration: an opening out and relaxing of the attention, allowing it to play freely with any idea which hovers in the vicinity of the chosen subject. Putting one's self into such a receptive and inquisitive frame of mind leads into unforeseen directions, and one should be prepared to ignore the boundaries which put limits on perception, dividing it into compartments labelled: 'artistic', 'scientific', 'philosophical', etc. This narrow, linear view can give way to a spherical outlook, in which being many-sided need not mean being a dilettante.

If there is a basic rule for such an outlook, it seems to be that the attention must be given a subject, a central point from which it can then go out, like the rings around a pebble dropped in water. The pebble must be dropped again and again, if the ring patterns are not to be lost in the surrounding waters: the subject acts like the pebble, and must be returned to repeatedly.

Time plays a vital role in this process, and only with time does it become possible to see the broad design made by the innumerable criss-crossing waves of attention.

Limitations of time and space dictated by the format of this book have allowed me to present only a very condensed and accelerated picture of what is actually an extremely slow process, but I hope that these notes and illustrations will act as a stimulus to the reader to explore the subjects in his own way. I have been asked by other artists why I should want to give away material that I ought to be keeping to myself, for my own use. The question is logical, but my answer is that I feel compelled to share creative experience, and do not feel any loss of identity in such sharing: if my experience can be used by others, it will be used in entirely different ways than I will use it myself. So nothing is lost, and someone may gain.

The choice of a subject is very important and very personal. A passing visual fancy will not do for the purpose of developing the faculty of seeing creatively. It must be a subject with which one feels a strong affinity, which excites the intellect as well as the senses, and which can be returned to over and over again without boredom. I have found that natural forms answer to all these requirements. No matter how simple it may seem at first glance, a natural form is always multi-dimensional: it is not only itself—leaf, stone, or whatever—but also part of the complex language of all nature. Any minute detail from it seems to give off sparks, ideas, links, comparisons—if you take the trouble to search that detail for clues. Since we also project ourselves upon what we see, no two people will interpret a natural form in the same way. But the intrinsic discipline of the natural form, along with its casual display of incredible variety, seems to act as a trigger to the imagination, simultaneously canalizing it and liberating it.

Figure 1   Waves in a tray of water

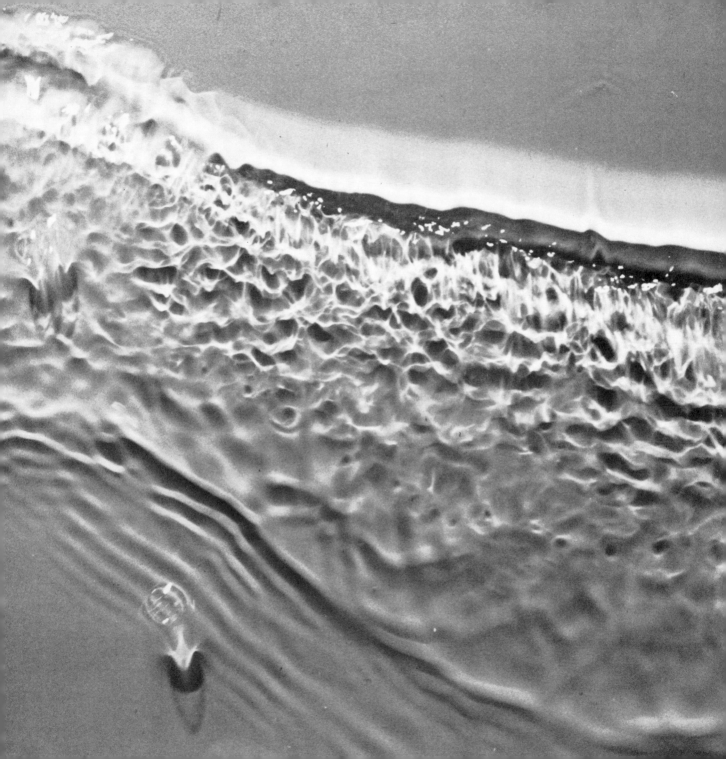

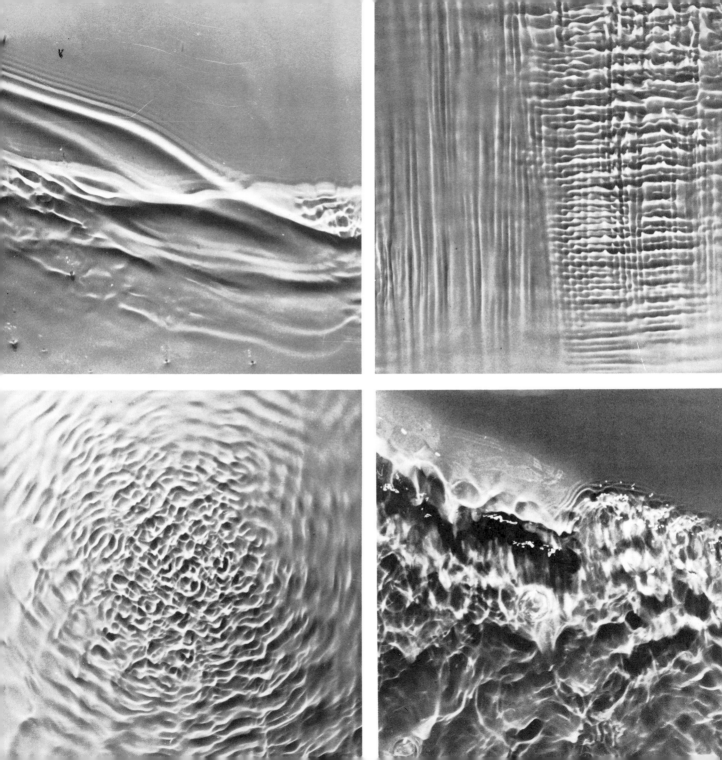

1 Water

I begin by looking at water as if I had never seen it before. This is not easy—it means seeing it only here and now, close at hand, unfamiliarly, questioningly. I fill a shallow pan with water and place it on the table before me. I give my whole attention to it, as if the water itself was being slowly poured into the mould of my mind.

I rock the pan from side to side, tap it, jiggle it, watching the ripples forming and vanishing. I blow on the water. I stir it with my hand and drag my fingers through it. I float small objects on the surface. I place the pan in bright light, in dim light, and observe the moving reflections in the water. I pour water into a deep glass bowl and watch the shape of the flickering liquid column, and the splash of water on water. I make bubbles in the water, blowing through a straw. I put a drop of ink in the bowl of water and watch it slowly descending, mushrooming. I put drops of water on a sheet of glass and observe them from beneath, running, joining together. I watch water boiling and examine steam clouds. I put ice cubes on a plate and look at them through a magnifying-glass. I play with ice, melting bits of it with hot water, adding new chunks, building with ice.

Gradually, my games take on the character of experiments, and I find that I want to isolate and develop some of the many impressions I have been collecting. Getting into the subject requires calm, relaxed, unhurried receptivity. But once you are really *with* your subject, an intense creative energy takes over, and the most ordinary facts become extraordinary: you do the washing-up, water the garden, take a bath, walk in the rain—in every form, water is suddenly speaking to you, showing you something you had never noticed, suggesting some idea for you to pursue. And it is important to pursue each idea. Not to be put off by a 'this has been done before', or 'but everybody knows that!' kind of attitude. Whatever it is that has been done before has not necessarily been done by you, in your own way, and is not necessarily 'known' by you, in your own way.

Figures 2–5   Water in motion

15

Waves

A series of photographs of waves made by rocking and vibrating the sides of a shallow pan of water, gives me the possibility of studying at leisure and in close-up some of the wave patterns I had observed earlier. (A strong overhead light will clearly show up ripple patterns, as you probably noticed in a swimming-pool or bathtub.)

Examining one of these photographs (Fig. 7) for some time, I gradually notice a very precise geometric design underlying the agitation of the waves. I begin a drawing on graph-paper (Fig. 6), imagining that I am looking down from a considerable height at a pattern of which the photograph would be only a detail. If you examine the right-hand corner of Fig. 7 and mentally extend the curves so that they form concentric circles, you will see how I arrived at my design. I notice that the crests of the waves occur at precise intervals, and with a compass I draw regularly spaced curves which bisect the circles, creating the 'troughs' of the waves. I emphasize these hollows by shading, then suddenly feel that I have seen this design somewhere before. Looking for examples I come across some striking and unexpected resemblances (pp. 18–19).

My excitement at this discovery is not dampened by the possibility that the territory has already been explored. In fact, I embark upon a hunt for whatever existing reference material might illuminate my chance finding. The search yields so much information (see p. 86: *Links and References*) that it appears I ought to have at least three lives: one to merely collect the material, one to absorb it all, and one to find out what I want it for. And I realize that if I am to move a step further with these experiments, I must limit my consumption of information to those items which excite my imagination, as the experience of seeing excites it. The accumulation of knowledge which one is not equipped to use creatively produces a sensation very similar to over-eating. I store away those morsels which I know will serve me in future, and return my attention to the pan of water, to the waves captured by the camera's eye, trying to keep alive the interplay of observation and intuition, vision and Vision.

Figure 6   Pencil drawing on graph-paper

17

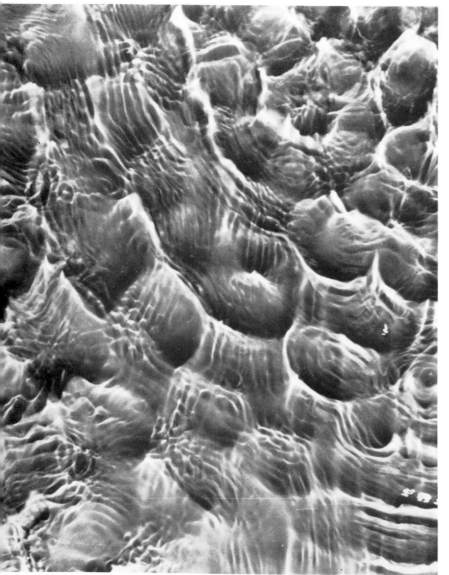

18

Figure 10   Plaster cast of pineapple skin
(see also p. 45)

Figure 11   Wave pattern formed by two
floats bobbing at the same frequency.
(Reproduced from What is Light?, by
A. C. S. van Heel and C. H. F. Velzel, by
courtesy of World University Library,
London).

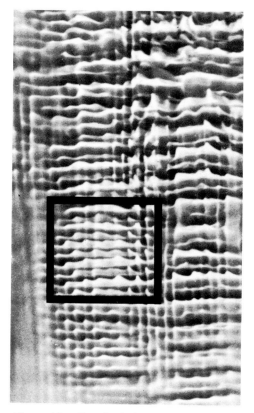

Figure 12   Detail of vibrating water

After making a tracing of a very small section of Fig. 12, and filling in the waves with ink (Fig. 13), I see that I have stumbled on another clue which may have some significance. The tracing shows the waves as a thickening of parallel lines, at irregular intervals. This leads me to a series of improvisations on wave profiles, such as Fig. 14, made by raising 'bumps' in parallel lines. Scattering these bumps over the lines in assymetrical arrangements leads to patterns which take on recognizable forms. Turn the book on its side, and you will see the bumpy lines of Fig. 16 transform themselves into a face. A well-known optical illusion and graphic device, but one which I have never considered in the context of *waves*. It starts off a chain of ideas and questions: in perceiving objects, are we simply 'filling in the blanks' between vibrations in space? Is space itself like a web of fine, taut strings, and every 'solid object' merely a succession of wave profiles, the vibrations of those strings? Fact or fantasy, the idea has a strong appeal to me and I pursue it through sketches and three-dimensional models. Is the specific shape of an object only a question of intervals, like the melody in music? No sooner does the music analogy come to mind than I want to see and hear the kind of sounds that a particular wave formation would make. On music-paper, I draw an enlarged version of Fig. 12, sprinkling dots, intended as notes, all along the waves' profiles (Fig. 15). Without means of testing the composition at once, I tentatively assign each bar of music to a voice-range, intending the piece to be hummed by ten voices. The sketch goes into my file of projects to be taken up when the necessary technical means are at hand. (In this case, ten singers at my disposition; and considerably more than my present rudimentary knowledge of musical form.)

The 'face' produced by slightly modifying parallel lines makes me wonder if the reverse would be feasible: face into wave pattern? I cut up a photograph into narrow strips and re-assemble them, taping the strips together in their proper order, but accordion-pleating them. The result (Fig. 16a) when viewed horizontally seems oddly three-dimensional, the face becoming a group of floating shapes advancing and receding. However, the tonality of the photograph prevents us from 'reading' the face as pattern. More to do with perception than with waves in water, of course, but then, should we separate what our eyes perceive from the mechanism which is perceiving it? You see the black signs you are now reading as words. But turn the book upside down, and you will see black signs, which may or may not be words. Which is the 'best' approach to the subject, words or signs? Face or wave pattern? If ever you feel that your explorations are leading you into areas which 'have nothing to do' with your subject, remember that it is not only the subject, water or whatever, but also your own perception of it which you are exploring.

Wanting to look further into the tonal quality of waves, I work on gouache studies in black, white and greys (Fig. 18), and on three-dimensional models in perspex, wood or cardboard (Fig. 19), where light itself creates double images or wave patterns.

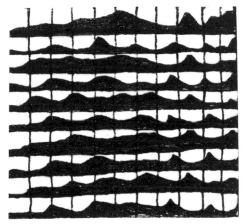

Figure 13   Tracing, from same detail

Figure 14   Drawing on scraperboard

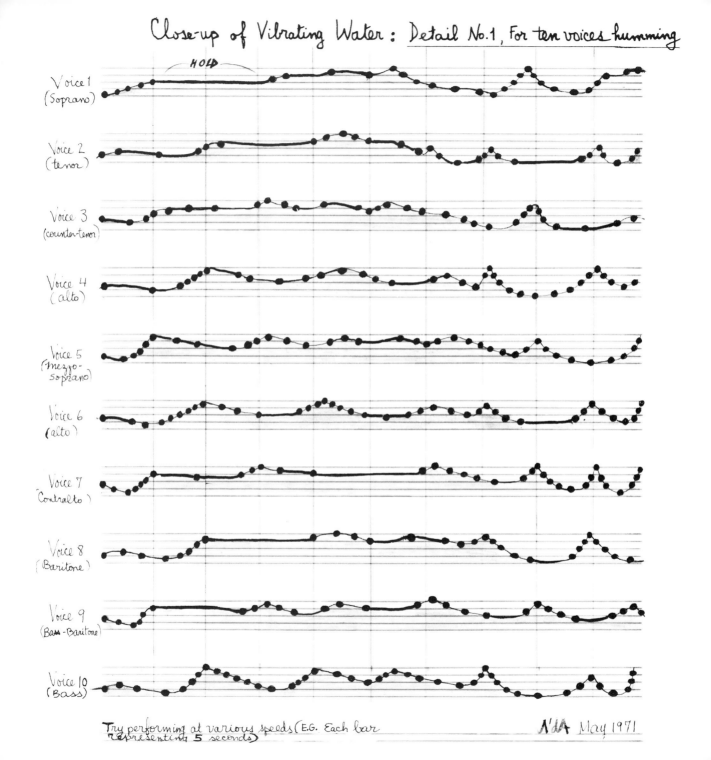

Figure 15   opposite   *Detail of vibrating water, interpreted as music*

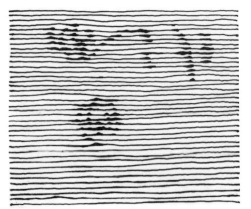

Figure 16   *Ripples or face? Ink drawing.* (Turn book on its side)

Figure 16a   *Face illusion. Pleated photograph*

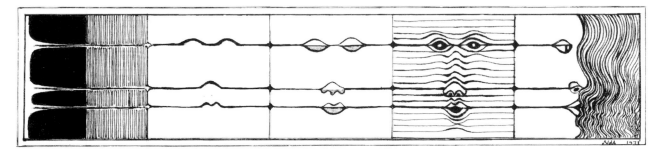

Figure 17   *'Waves into face into waves'. Ink drawing*

Figure 18 opposite *Gouache study of waves*

Figure 19 *Cardboard model* 'Light waves'

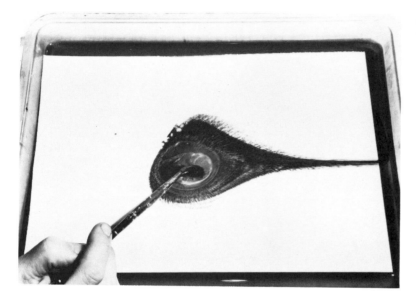

Figure 20   Drawing on water (card just below the surface). First image

Figure 21   Modification of first image

Floating

I examine the characteristics of things seen under water and floating on it. Watching drops of Indian ink lying on the surface, curling into whorls and arabesques, then slowly sinking in the water, I decide to record some of the patterns of this movement by experimenting with the simple fact that a liquid which will float on the surface of water can also be 'imprinted' or offset onto paper, cardboard, etc., as the ancient process of marbling illustrates. (If you have never associated marbled paper with moving water, compare Fig. 22 with the photographs of waves.)

Not wishing to arrive at the decorative patterns obtained by standard marbling techniques, and using only ink and water, I improvise and eventually chance upon a method of actually drawing *on* water, a sheet of cardboard floating just below the surface (Figs. 20, 21). If a piece of dry paper is placed over the floating image, that image can be lifted out between the two sheets, like a sandwich. But this requires considerable trial and error as the ink tends to float right off the card. Salt added to water makes it denser so the ink will float longer without sinking. Talcum powder sprinkled over water makes an almost impermeable surface from which the ink can be picked up without wetting the paper at all, but you lose the subtle edges of ink-on-water shapes. Milk floating on water makes a good surface which can be drawn onto quite easily with any pointed instrument.

Such technical recreations are, I feel, just that. In the context of a profound involvement with one's subject, they become a means of relaxing—a way of being attentive but without thought or conscious intention. I personally do not attach any particular exclusivity to most of the results thus obtained, but they can, occasionally, produce a 'mandala'-like image, one which has the power to stimulate a meditative state. A state often induced by the contemplation of natural forms or processes themselves—clouds, flickering flames, puddles of water, etc. Anyone who can see the 'mandala' kind of image in a cloud or a coffee-stain can also, in my opinion, manipulate random methods of producing such images, if shown examples of these methods. Whether the results are Art or not is a matter of opinion, but I do not think that the techniques ought to be kept secret.

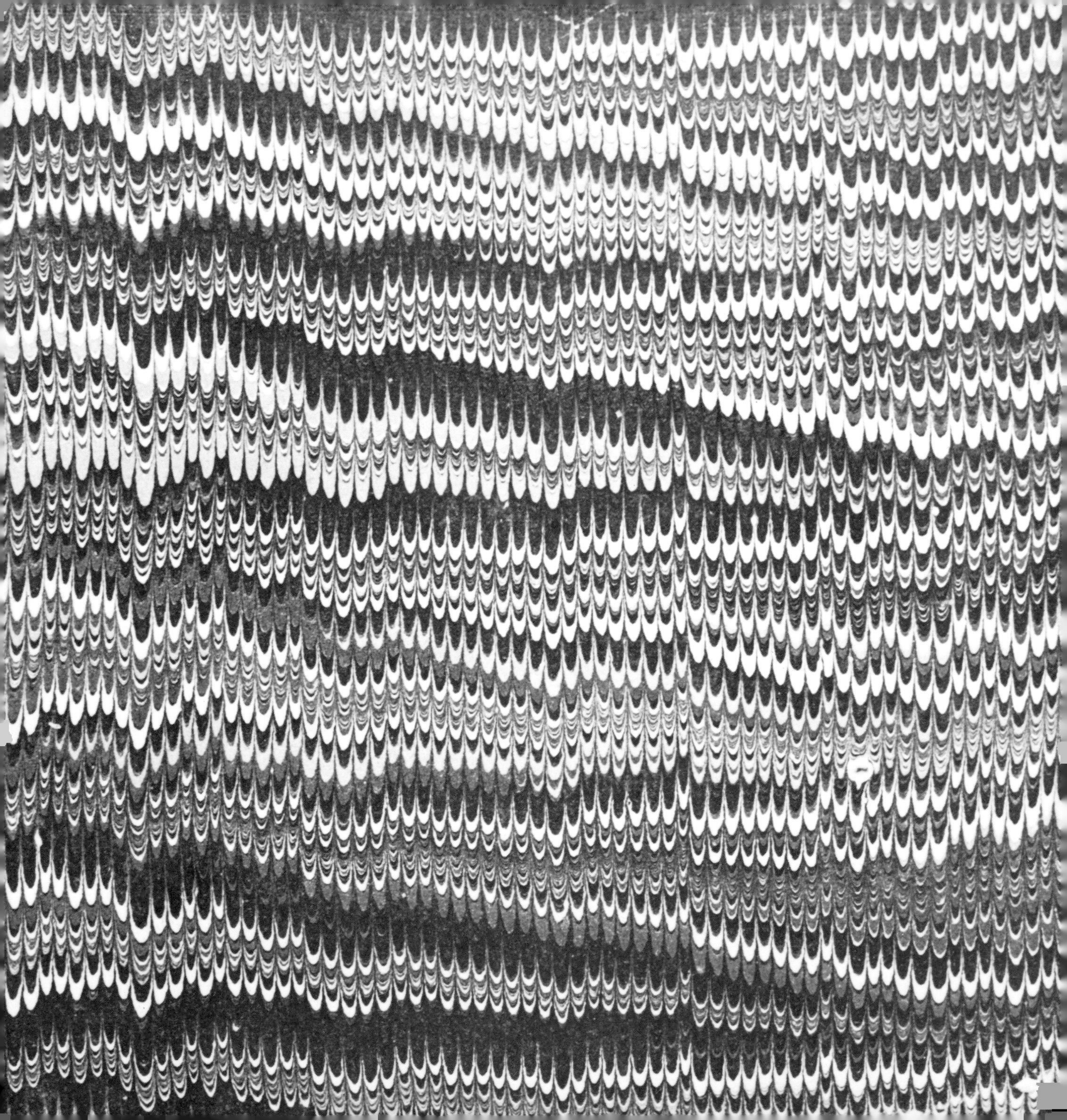

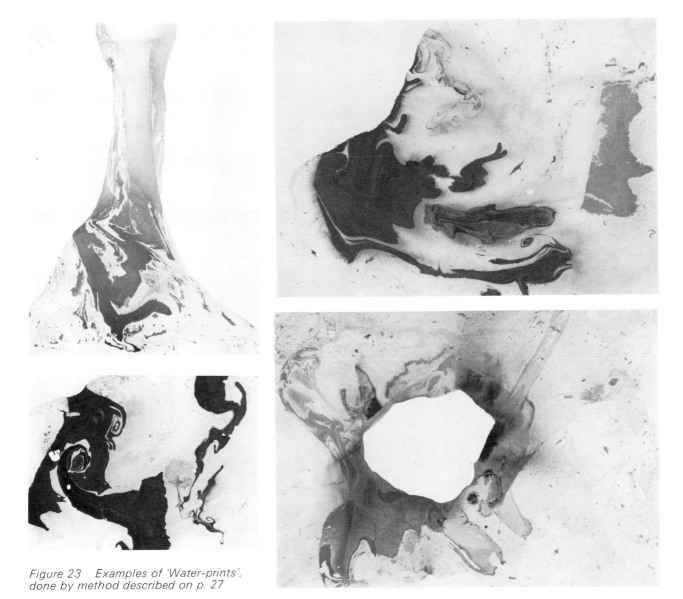

Figure 22   opposite   *Marbled end-paper, from a nineteenth-century book*

Figure 23   *Examples of 'Water-prints', done by method described on p. 27*

Bubbles

A film of soap on water. Air introduced into the film by blowing through a straw. The film stretching without breaking into hundreds of iridescent globes: bubbles. What could be more familiar? Yet, there is enough in this one small natural event to fill a lifetime of creative experiment. It occupies only a very few of these pages, as an offshoot to the observation of water, but even a short period of time spent closely watching bubbles under various conditions can become an illuminating experience.

I devise various methods of blowing bubbles, to obtain different formations. For instance: taping several lengths of plastic tubing to a flat piece of wood, making a sort of organ-pipe.

I build a bubble-watching container, by drilling a hole in the lid of a screw-top jar, inserting a plastic tube, and sealing the edges of the hole. The bubbles last a long time in this jar, allowing me to work on pencil and watercolour studies, details of bubble-construction seen from every possible angle.

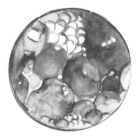

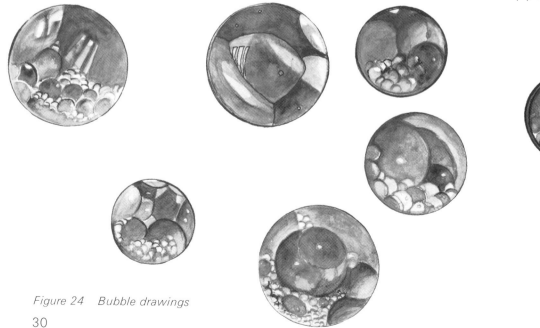

Figure 24   Bubble drawings

30

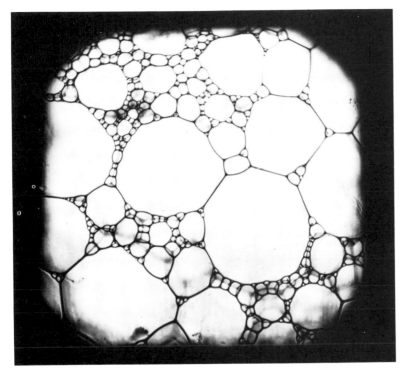

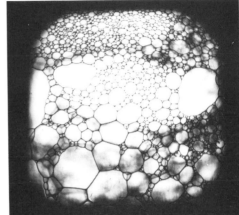

Figures 25 and 26   Projected bubbles

I experiment with projected bubbles: fortunately, my slide-projector has a space of about three-quarter inches between the slide-carrier and the lens, just right for inserting a 'trough' made of thin glass cut to size. A few drops of soapy water, a bit of plastic tubing to blow through, and my device is ready for trial. I fill the trough with bubbles and switch the projector on: the device works. Impossible in black and white (Figs. 25, 26) to give anything but the roughest idea of the beauty of projected bubbles, and the fascination of watching their constantly changing colours and patterns. I can only urge you to try this experiment, or any variation on it, for yourself. In a completely darkened room, the bubbles' rainbow colours and three-dimensional structure will show up better if you place a cardboard disc with a tiny hole in the centre over the projector lens.

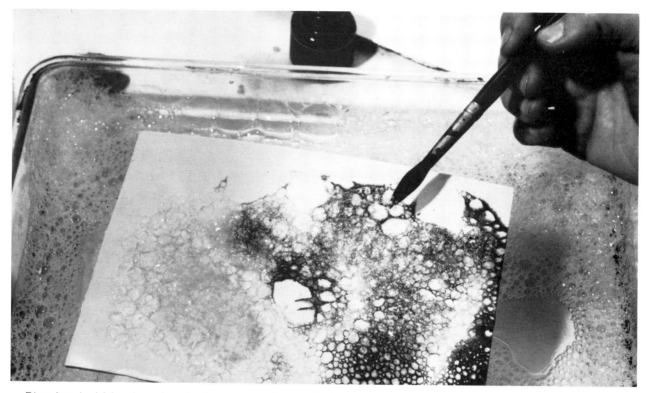

Blowing bubbles in a bowl of soapy water until they over-
flow, growing over the sides and spreading out onto a piece of
paper on the table, I notice that faint traces of their structure are
left behind on the paper after the bubbles disintegrate. Wanting
to see these traces more clearly, I add ink to the soapy water
and blow into it again, thus discovering what I name the
'Bubble-Tracks' technique. A variation on it is demonstrated in
Fig. 27. It consists of picking up a layer of suds onto a sheet of
card, and lightly touching the edges of the bubbles with a
brush barely tipped with ink. Any pattern left behind by the
bursting ink-and-soap bubbles is pleasing to look at, but a
certain amount of selection and control does enter into deciding
how to place the pattern, how much of it to ink, etc.

Figure 27   'Bubble-Tracks' technique

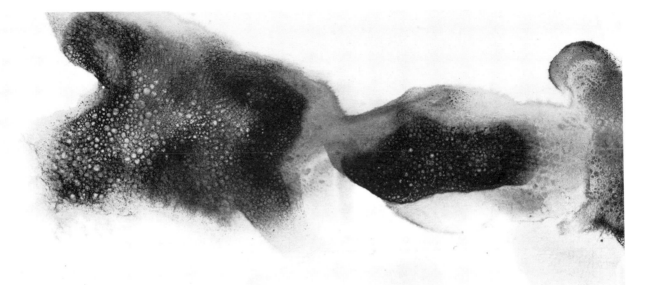

Figures 28 and 29   *Bubble-Tracks*

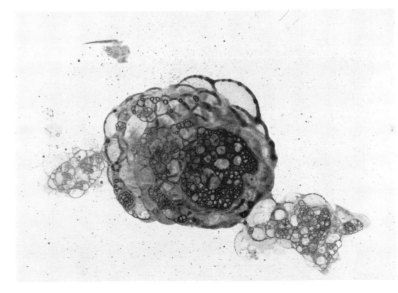

Reflections

I paint an enamelled basin black, fill it with water, and settle down for a long look into the reflections. I find that it is almost impossible to focus simultaneously on the various levels which I see. I try to define these by painting a white square on the bottom of the basin, floating a small piece of wood on the water, and resting a box on the edge of the basin. There still remains the reflected levels, which interpenetrate the 'real' levels in a most bewildering manner: now you see it, now you don't. The diagram, Fig. 30, illustrates this:

Level 1   Top surface of the box.
Level 2   Surface of water.
Level 3   Floor of the basin.
Level 4   The 'deepest' illusory level, which is the reflected ceiling of the room.

Each of the reflections which I can see has its own level, and creates a sense of endless space, a frame-within-a-frame. To explore these depths, I begin an extended study of reflections in a bathtub, the water coloured by bath-salts (Fig. 31). The high ceiling and narrow walls of the bathroom are clearly reflected in the still, green water. Attempting to indicate the depth of the reflections, the surface texture of the water, as well as the solidity of the bathtub itself, is a task demanding un-swerving attention. I would highly recommend it as a device to heighten awareness. You might say: why not take a photo-graph and save yourself all that trouble? For some purposes, this would be sufficient. But in the context of our experiments, the process is more important than the end-product. In the slow, gradual penetration of reality we gain access to the deeper, more intangible levels of perception, where our creative resources and limitations may be seen. If, after spend-ing considerable time on such a demanding exercise as, say, painting reflections, you find that you do not like the result *as a painting*, you can throw the painting away. But the experience of that pin-pointed attention cannot be lost. It has been distilled into your mind and will certainly emerge at some time, perhaps in a completely different form.

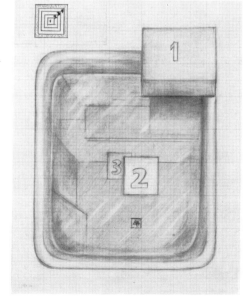

Figure 30

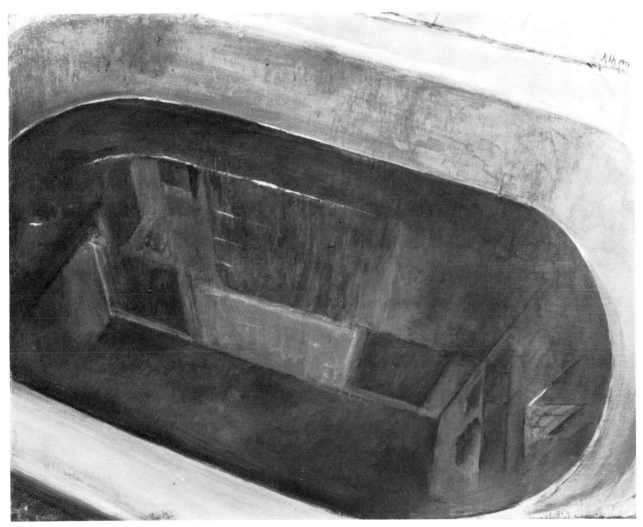

Figure 31   Reflections in bathtub.
Acrylic on canvas

Ice

With a tray of ice cubes, a cup of hot water and an eye-dropper, I make ice sketches, re-freeze them then modify them further. It is like playing with solid light. I 'sculpt' water, pouring it into trays which I have divided by means of plasticine walls into various shapes, sometimes adding coloured inks to the water before freezing it. I introduce bubbles into chunks of ice. I freeze a few drops of water between two thin pieces of glass and project this slide; the crystalline structure of the ice becomes apparent. Burrowing grooves and tunnels into ice cubes with the aid of hot water, the idea of a translucent sculpted wall gradually emerges, and I begin a series of maquettes for this project. From ice-models, I move on to clay, then plaster-casts (Figs. 33, 34), then resin casts (Fig. 35). I investigate glass-melting procedures, making tests in a small enamelling kiln, perfectly adequate for the purpose. I experiment with casting in resin and find it very suitable for translating my ice-models into more permanent form, particularly the clear 'embedding' type of resin (see Materials, p. 95).

Playing with ice floating on water, I improvise some variations on the 'Water-Prints' method (described on p. 27), drawing directly onto thin slivers of ice with Indian ink. I freeze thick soap-suds in a glass jar, then, touching the edges with ink, I can observe the fine filigree patterns of frozen bubbles. I discover a most absorbing and hypnotic occupation: touching chunks of ice with ink, as they slowly melt on a sheet of blotting paper. The ink spreads out around them in waves, making the most intricately shaded patterns (more interesting when they are actually in the process of forming than in the final, static result). One can quite easily spend several hours simply watching this event happening. The effect is fleeting but sufficiently stimulating to provoke the imagination to go further. Technical means of prolonging such effects can always be found if one wants to find them.

Figure 32   opposite   *Ice-cube 'wall'*

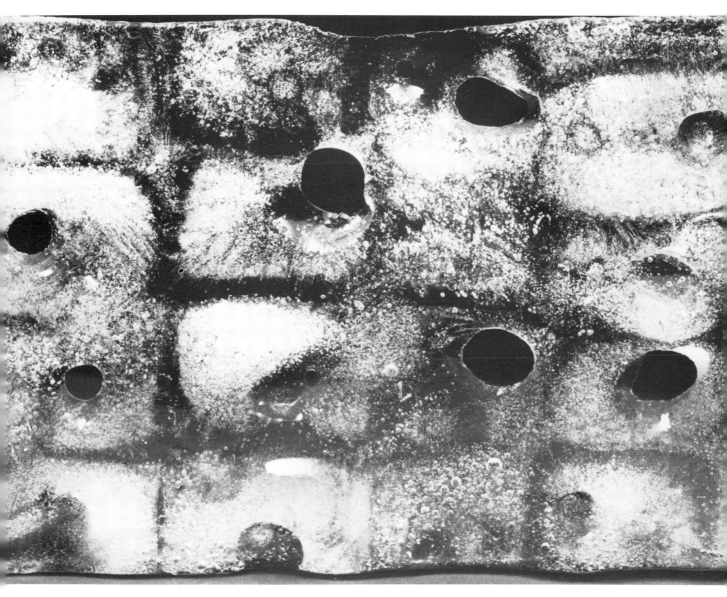

Figure 33   Plaster mould (detail) for 'ice-wall' maquette

Figure 34   Plaster cast from above mould

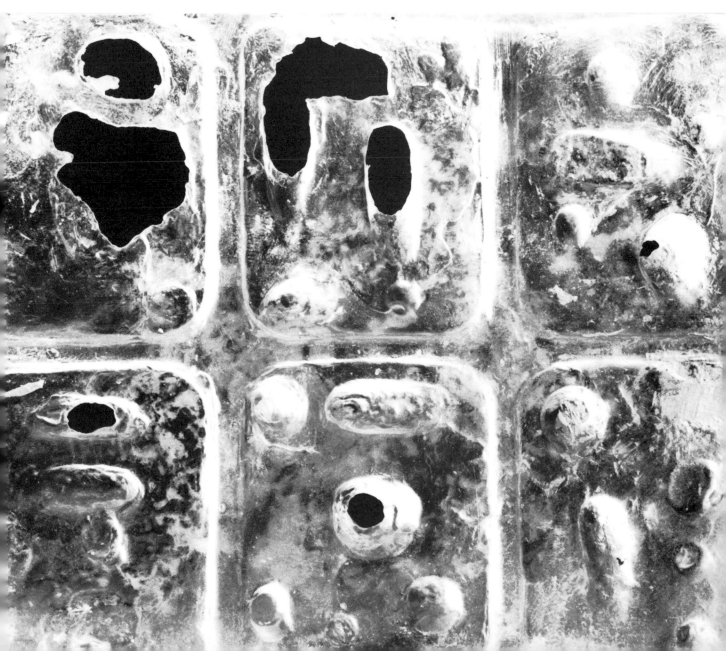

Figure 35   Detail of transparent resin cast

Summing-up

If considerable time has been spent studying a subject and following up the various directions it may have led to, it is a good idea to pause at some stage and review the work done thus far. As an example, I drew the following diagram, which illustrates the 'pebble dropped in water' character of the different points of view which concentration on the theme of water suggested to me, each 'splash' or idea producing its own continuing reverberations.

Waves
1   Waves seen as forming geometric pattern. Similar design found in other natural forms and processes.
2   Waves seen as precisely spaced modifications of parallel lines. Analogy with graphic patterns, and musical form.
3   Waves seens as musical pattern, or vibrations in space. Questions about perception. Do we see wave patterns or objects?
4   Waves seen as three-dimensional, transparent bands of alternating light and shade.

Floating   Ink-on-water methods as a means of recording movement on the surface of water. Accidental processes as imagination-stimulators.

Bubbles   Water observed in its ability to act as membrane and lens. Methods of observing the colour and structure of bubbles.

Reflections   Reflections in water seen as a means of exercising the mind, through focusing simultaneously on the various levels perceived.

Ice   Water seen as solid light, a material for modelling.

In a separate section, pp. 86–90, I have listed and commented upon some of the other directions which my observations led me to.

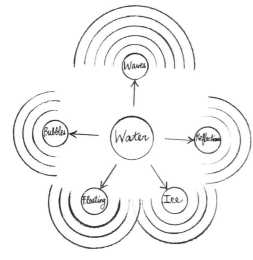

Figure 36

Figure 37   Drops of water on glass

2 Pineapple

From the initial love-at-first-sight fascination with a specific natural form comes a desire to assimilate its every detail, possess it somehow. Actors are sometimes taught to 'make like' a tree, or a stone, or a chair. This approach is just as valid for our purposes. Drawing from life can be in visual terms what mime is to the actor. In this context, drawing ought to be considered in the same sense as in drawing water from a well. That is, extracting from the subject you are drawing those elements which move you the most.

There is something about the texture and pattern of the pineapple skin, the spikiness of the leaves, the 'pineappleness', that I want to grasp in a precise and thorough way. I begin by a series of close-up drawings (Figs. 39, 40, 41), in which the emphasis is on the regularly spaced peaks. This leads me back inevitably to waves (Fig. 42, and compare p. 44 with p. 18), and to further investigations along the intricate path of analogies and comparisons, but it would require another volume to even scratch the surface of these aspects. (Some are mentioned on pp. 91–92.)

I carefully strip a section of skin from the pineapple and make plaster casts of both the inner and outer faces (Fig. 43, and Fig. 10 on p. 19). When the fruit pulp is scraped away from the skin, the tiny wells, which form the peaks on the other side, are revealed. There is something peculiarly satisfying about this simple and perfectly regular pattern, and its possibilities as a starting point for applied design ideas are so numerous that I begin a notebook for such ideas, while at the same time continuing my observations and studies. Working in this way, you become aware of an element of growth, parallel to the process of evolution in nature: the fittest of your ideas will survive, the others will drop away of their own accord, but each stage is valid as a preparation for the next. Sometimes it is only by repeating a step many times, with only slight variations, that you can see what you yourself are after. You may find that it is much less than you thought. Perhaps you won't need the pineapple at all, only the hexagonal pattern of its skin. But the close rapport between yourself and the subject causes you to recognize a particular theme which is your own. Wanting to follow the spiralling path of the scales (or *florets*, to be exact)

Figure 38   Close-up of pineapple

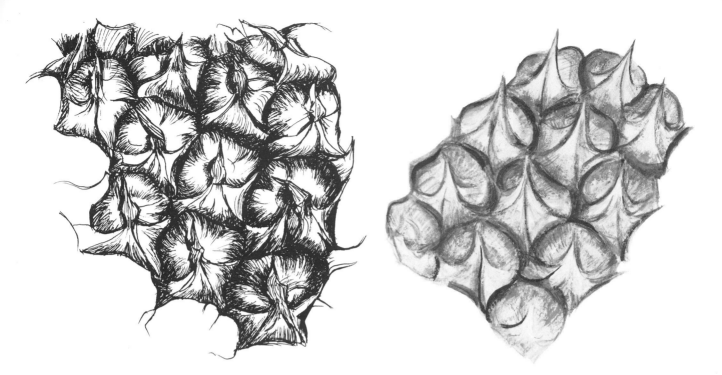

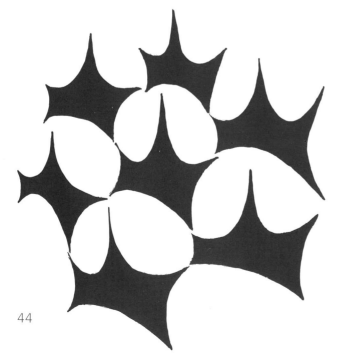

Figures 39–41   Drawings. Pineapple-
skin peaks

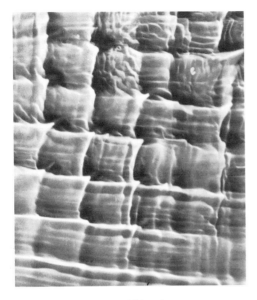

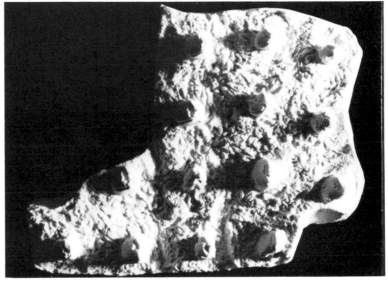

Figure 42 above *Vibrating water*

Figure 43 above right *Plaster mould Inner face of pineapple skin*

Figure 44 right *Pineapple skin, cleaned of fruit-pulp*

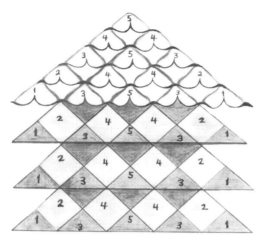

Figure 45   Pineapple triangles. Pencil and ink on graph paper

right round the pineapple, I find that this is impossible without some means of identifying each of them. I therefore paint numbers on each scale, from one to five, making a rule that those which point corner to corner will have like numbers, while those which are at right angles to each other will have unlike numbers. I end up with the following arrangement (making a grand total of 112 scales):

Three rows of 5's (with 5 scales in each row).
Five rows of 4's (with 6 scales in three of them, and 5 scales in the other two).
Five rows of 3's (with 6 scales in three of them, and 5 scales in the other two).
Five rows of 2's (with 5 scales in four of them, and 4 scales in the remaining row).
Three rows of 1's (with 6 scales in two of them, and 5 scales in the remaining row).

Looking at this numbered pineapple, I then draw a kind of projection of it (Fig. 46), as if I were standing at the centre and could pull the shell around me. If you mentally join the loose ends shown in the drawing, you can reconstruct the whole pineapple. Or open it out further, visualizing it as a giant carpet.

If you are interested in the symbolic associations of numbers and geometric patterns, the hexagonal symmetry of the pineapple skin provides a starting point for what could be a long-term project (see No. 29 in the *Links and References* list).

Using only a triangular section of my numbered pineapple as a model, I work on a drawing of superimposed triangular planes (Fig. 45), and others consisting of overlapping rectangles, each measuring five 'scales' by five (Fig. 47).

Because all natural forms have an intrinsic mathematical order, it is not unlikely that anyone who observes and draws from nature will come up with some sort of geometric style. But I would like to emphasize the importance of recognizing the difference between this natural evolution and the approach which instantly translates the forms of nature into 'designs' or 'abstract patterns'. We are trying to be as attentive as possible to the subject, both for its own qualities, and as a means of putting in motion the process of creativity in ourselves. This is

Figure 46   Pencil drawing on graph paper. Numbered pineapple

Figure 47 'Pineappleness'. *Pencil on graph paper*

quite different from a stylizing which imposes the conventions of a particular school upon a form. Nor does it bear much relationship to that approach which reduces things to their nearest geometric shapes, as a useful technique for mastering the difficulties of drawing from life. The distinction may be a subtle one, but it is significant and necessary to our research: we do not aim to *master* the subject, but simply abandon ourselves to it, all our faculties attuned to it. We do not impose pre-conceived rules upon it, but try to discover a rule within it which can serve us as a guide to the maze of creative possibilities within ourselves.

After doing many detailed drawings of the pineapple leaves, I find that I want to isolate the qualities of spikiness and subtle tonal gradation. I remove a few of the newest leaves from the heart of the pineapple top, and arrange these on a plain white background. With this arrangement as a model, I work on a series of drawings and three-dimensional compositions. The relief versions, consisting of cut-out shapes in a white surface placed at a slight distance away from an equally white background, produce the finely graduated shadows which I was after.

There is no reason why composing with pineapple leaves— or any other parts of natural forms—should be any less valid than composing with man-made design modules such as cubes, spheres, wire, dots, lines.

Innumerable examples of modular units can be found in natural forms (see p. 74), and if one doesn't particularly care about the permanence of sketches or rough models, it is possible to do without the usual art-materials entirely, for purposes of working out visual ideas.

The distinct individuality of nature's materials, plus the fact that most of them alter in shape and colour fairly rapidly, makes them suspect from a purist point of view. However, we do live in a world shaped largely by natural forces and it would be a challenge to the imagination to use these forces and forms directly.

The dried pineapple skin shown in Fig. 50 is the same piece which you saw in its fresh state in Fig. 44. Time has transformed the neat, simple geometry of its youth into a convoluted,

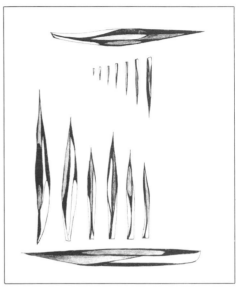

Figure 48   left   Pineapple top. Ink study

Figure 49   Composition based on pineapple leaves. Ink drawing

baroque kind of order. Here is the start of another long-term visual thesis: find links between the art and architecture of various periods in history and the forms of ageing or decay as seen in nature. (Do grotesque or very ornate styles in art go with a general sense of decadence, of 'dying', in a civilization?) Compare the 'styles' of natural forms in a state of advanced age with styles in art: what happens to lines, to shapes, to colours? You could take a drawing of very simple geometric form and pure colour (for example, based on the pineapple skin) through successive 'ageing' modifications: the shapes curling in upon themselves, the colour becoming mellower, losing its separateness from other colours. A technique used in animation-drawing would be useful here: draw over a light-box, on sheets of paper thin enough so that you can always see the previous drawing beneath the one you are working on. And try the reverse procedure, taking a very 'aged', intricate design backwards, to its lines of origin. Size would play an important part: think of the pineapple, shrunken with age into a tiny brown object, the symmetry of its design no longer discernible but nonetheless, still there, transformed.

Figure 50   Dried pineapple skin

3 The Hand

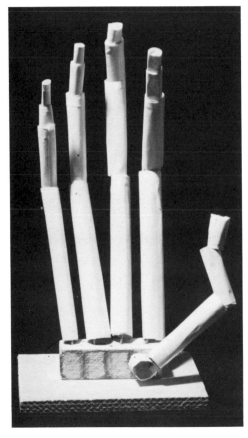

Figure 51   Hand model. Paper and wire

Think of the combinations possible with a pair of objects which are mirror-images of each other, having five mobile, jointed units each, textured with a distinctive, precise pattern of indented lines. Construct such objects, even if only from a verbal description of their characteristics, and you are sure to come up with a most ingenious and versatile design system. Little wonder that the hand is such a universally accepted symbol, whether simply of the human presence ('I was here'), or of measurement, proportion, direction, warning, destiny. The hands' power of expression, sometimes condensing into a single gesture a subtle gamut of emotions, is a theme which deserves a book in itself. My own experiments on the following pages approach the hand only as a kind of portable landscape, distinct from its function as part of human anatomy. If you stop thinking of a hand as part of someone's portrait, it immediately becomes much easier to see its structure and mechanics.

I examine my own hand, group and regroup the fingers, stretch the skin of the palm or wrinkle it, make a fist and slowly open it, touch the tips of my fingers to each other, observe the movement of bones beneath the skin. I make a very simple model out of rolled paper over a wire armature (Fig. 51). Bending the wire at the joints, I look at the model from different angles and I begin to see it as architecture.

From many sketches, an idea for a group of buildings emerges —a research centre—based on the form of the hand, both for its symbolic and functional associations ('destiny' and 'handiwork'). Each of the towers would house activities of relevance to the future of man, symbolized by the 'lines of destiny' of the palm, which in this case would be the garden or forecourt of the buildings. I do not think you should reject such ideas, if they come up in the course of your research, as being too far removed from the realm of possibility. It may be an opportunity to see how far you are prepared to stretch the limits of 'possibility' within yourself.

With close-up views of the hand as a starting point, I work on drawings, paintings and constructions. The distinctly human characteristics of the hand make it difficult to see in the same way as one would see a stone or a mountain, but I want to avoid sentimental, or even surrealist interpretations without sacrificing the sensuousness of the form.

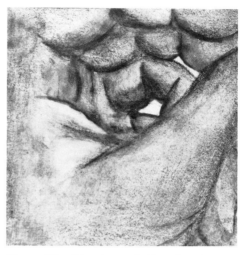

Figure 52   left   First maquette. Project for a research centre

Figure 53   'Handscape'. Pencil and watercolour

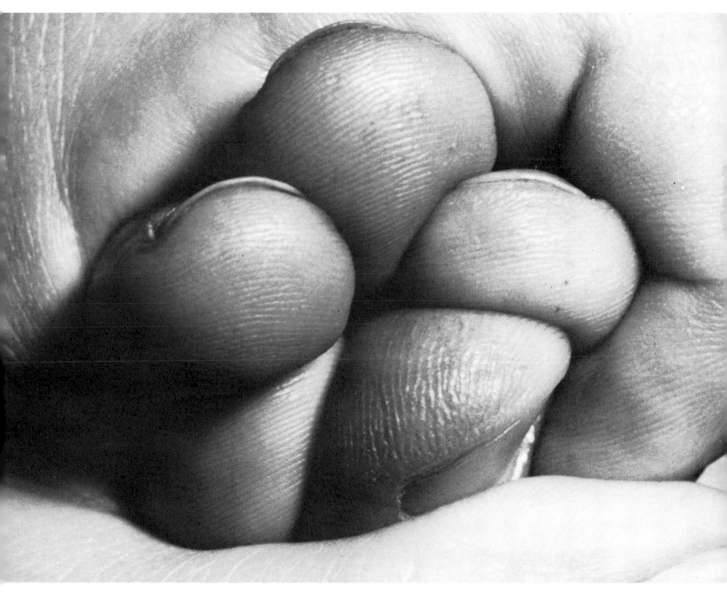

Figure 54   Fingers of one hand held in the other

I begin making plaster casts directly from the hand, in my attempts to remove it from everyday experience. This seems to work, insofar as the plaster, while retaining the tracks of human presence, transforms it into an unfamiliar, impersonal object.

Pouring plaster into a model's cupped hands, I am astonished to discover the shell-like shape (Fig. 56) of this mould (oil paint was rubbed in to bring out the texture). I begin to consider all the possible negative shapes obtainable by making moulds of the hollow spaces between two hands. Dipping my hands into a basin of water, I realize that I could just as easily dip them into a bowl of plaster and hold them in the desired position until the plaster was set.

Figure 55   Plaster cast of my left palm

Figure 56   What is it?

Figure 57 left Plaster cast from mould shown in Figure 56 (two cupped hands)

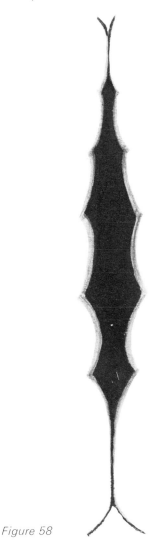

The hollow space between two hands folded in the 'praying' position is shown in Fig. 58 as a flat shape. But if you draw an outline of the hands around it, that shape instantly ceases to exist: it becomes a 'hollow'. With this idea in mind and with only my two hands as model, I try to find out more about the complex subject of negative and positive space, allied to the principle of 'left' and 'right' shapes or patterns. Putting the heel of my left hand flat against a mirror, I see the lines of the palm resolve themselves into a symmetrical pattern with their right-handed mirror image. I rub wet clay into my palms and press them down onto black paper to make direct handprints, from which I take only the linear patterns and develop them in prints and drawings. The close-up texture of the skin of the palm becomes important to me: I follow the wave formations of a single fingerprint, extending them into large drawings. I make fingerprint-slides on glass and project them, sometimes superimposing one slide over another.

Figure 58

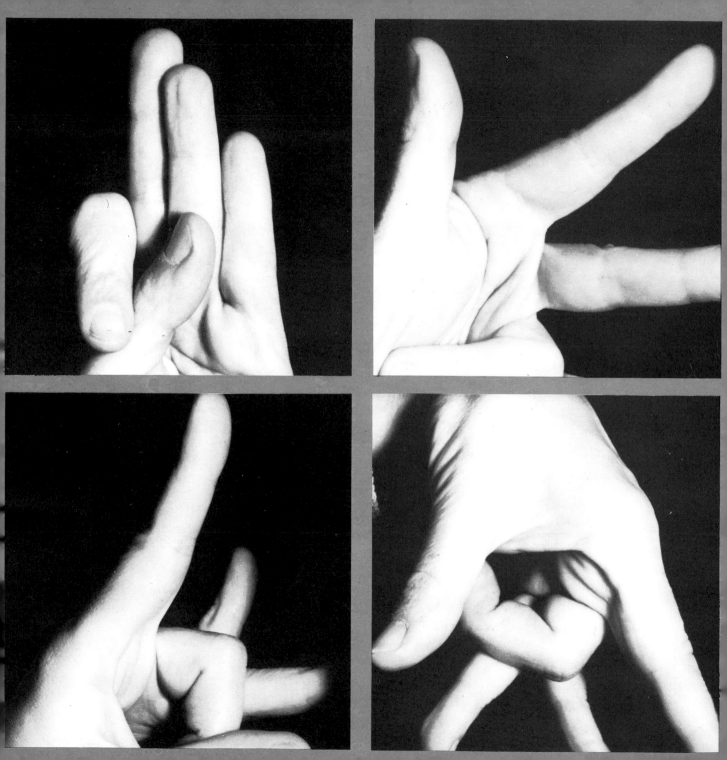

I make a small cardboard frame and place my hand behind it, arranging my fingers in as many different positions as I can think of, and I find this simple device sufficient to set off a whole chain of ideas, to be carried out in graphic and three-dimensional media. Some of the hand-behind-frame arrangements which I found to be most useful and conducive to further development are shown on the next few pages. Try placing a tiny cardboard frame over some of these photographs, to single out details. For example, on Figs. 61 and 62, note the shape of the hollow made by the third finger curled against the thumb. Compare it with Fig. 64, which is the shadow-shape of the whole hand.

Figure 63 'Hand-spaces'. *Ink drawings*

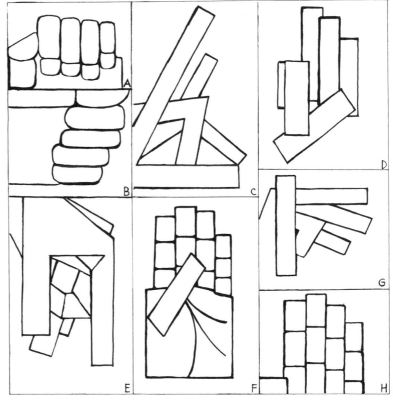

*Figures 64–67 opposite Hand
shadows behind translucent screen*

*Figures 68–70 Fingers stretching
muslin*

Figures 71 and 72   Hand in striped glove

A glove on which stripes have been painted provides a way of following the convolutions of the hand form as it moves within its box-frame. I remember waves, and think of the stripes as *filling* the space occupied by my hand rather than simply lying on the surface of it. Consider the idea that the hand contains all the basic-design principles: simply by placing your fingertips in various relationships to each other you create *points*. These can be joined by *lines* (you can stretch elastic bands or string between fingers). These, by the addition of sides, can be turned into *planes*. Which, taken all together, will constitute a *volume*, containing empty space. If you were to investigate each of these possibilities, with only your own hand to go by, you could confidently say at the end of your research that you had taken a very good foundation course in basic design.

A sheet of glass covered with tracing paper (or any thin paper), placed in cross-lighting will show small, ghostly spheres, like planets floating in space, when you press your fingertips against the back of the glass (Figs. 73, 74). In fact, if you look at your fingertips alone, ignoring the rest of the hand, and move them about so that they advance or recede in space, astronomy naturally comes to mind—constellations, charts of the heavens—even astrology, and the incredible figures it 'sees' as made up of the lines which join the dots which are the stars in the sky.

Mathematical games and geometric figures have been derived from time immemorial by simply arranging the fingers in various ways (see No. 45, in the list of *Links and References*). Then there is the vast field of using the hand as an object itself. A very crowded field indeed, but you could try to forget for a while about all the rings, bracelets, gloves, nail-varnishes, body-paint, etc., that you have seen, and start from scratch, just to see what happens. Or set yourself some specific task: what about functional jewellery? If you can make rings that project six inches from the fingers and play Strauss, why can't you make rings that peel potatoes? Challenge the imagination, on all levels.

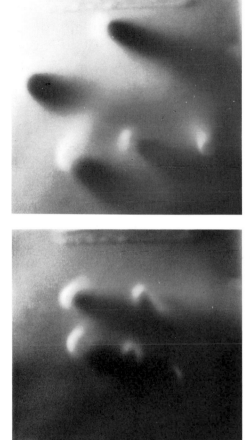

Figures 73 and 74   Fingertips pressed against translucent glass

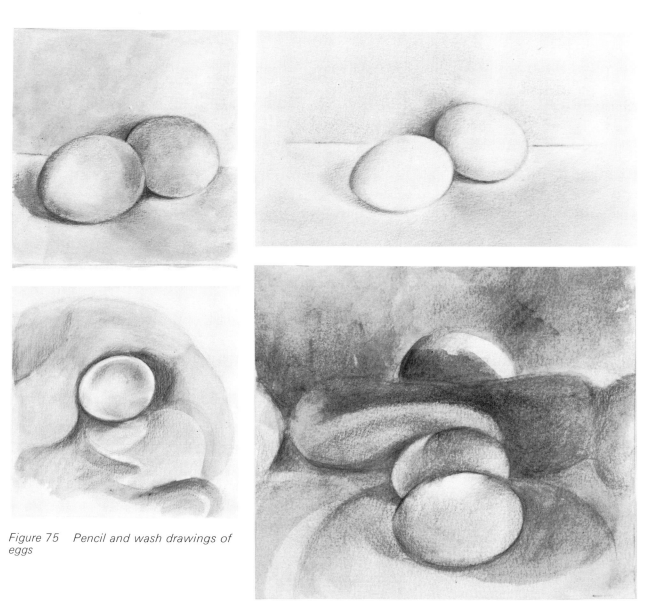

Figure 75   Pencil and wash drawings of
eggs

4 Eggs

When I use the word 'research' in connection with the experiments in this book, I am speaking of a poetic rather than a scientific approach to the accumulation of bits and pieces of visual and verbal information about a subject. To imprison the poetry in a too objective, scientific mould, would be to produce only hybrids: neither poetry nor science.

Perhaps the solution lies in using poetic means in one's research, not being afraid to question the subject imaginatively, boldly, even if this means transforming its normal characteristics. The poetic vision does not emerge all at once. The same slow, tentative probing that the scientist must practice can suddenly produce the 'Eureka!', the explosion of inspiration which makes it all worthwhile. But in our case, free from the scientific commitment to fact, we can assemble the material we collect from nature as a poet assembles his words. What is to stop us from declaring, for instance: 'The egg is sun's eye, the egg's son's in the sky?' Who's to disprove it? If we need proof, we can always draw a picture. But the poetic reality is not haphazard or disorderly. It has laws as strict as those of nature, laws that can sometimes be discovered by the simple transposition of natural laws into another context.

What do I want from you, egg? I am not sure. I can make a still-life of you, lying in a bowl on a kitchen table. I can make a six-foot high bronze version of you. I can paint you surrealistically, hanging limply from a tree. I can decorate you with faces or flowers or geometric patterns. I can think about your function: you are an embryo in a protective shell. Or I can just look at you, one egg alone, a group of eggs.

I begin with simple observations, pencil studies of eggs in light and shadow. I find that the perfect, impersonal shape of the egg makes it an ideal object for light's powers of transformation. It can seem round, flat, convex, concave. A mirror behind an egg pulls and stretches the shape into infinity. Shadows cast onto eggs from various objects produce completely new objects, phantom eggs.

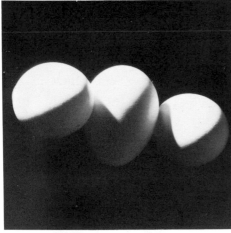

Figures 76 and 77   Eggs and shadows

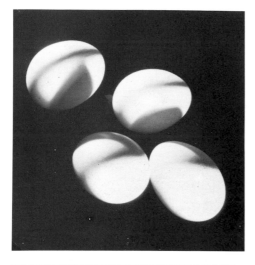

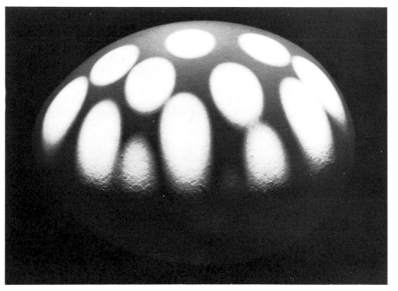

Figures 78 and 79   Eggs and shadows

Figures 80–83   opposite and right
Eggs with shadows cast by wires, etc.

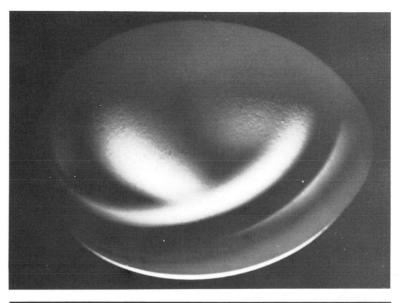

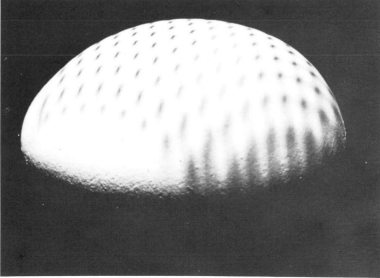

Figure 84   Eggshells on mirror

A row of half-shells standing on a mirror (Fig. 84) produces a strange image, logical yet somehow impossible. (Also look at it vertically.) The gaps between the two sets of open shells absorb my attention, calling it back to the hollows between cupped hands. I find that the kind of shapes made in space by placing eggs very close to each other but not touching (Fig. 85), is as significant to me as the solid form of the egg itself. The camera of the eye is not impartial, it selects only what it needs. But perhaps one is not aware of having made a choice until all the 'stills' are lined up next to each other. It then becomes possible to discern the direction or pattern of one's *seeing*, which includes moments of perception that took place long ago.

Figure 85   Two eggs and a space
between

I construct a miniature stage on which to arrange groups of eggs against different backgrounds and lighting effects. The group shown in Fig. 86 is in front of a sheet of mirror-foil, curved against the walls of the box/stage. The egg with a 'window' in it was blown, and suspended on a thread from the ceiling of the stage. It spun round slowly and continually which, with its curved reflected image, created a sense of expanding and contracting space. I tried backgrounds of stark white walls, coloured walls, partitions, steps, trompe-l'oeuil perspective, etc. The effect of placing the eggs on a stage immediately gave them another scale, and I could imagine tiny figures walking about in a dream-like, but possible environment. Drawing directly onto the photograph (Fig. 87), I tried to visualize such an environment.

I thought of these egg-forms as being sometimes translucent, allowing one to glimpse an inner structure. And sometimes opaque, with openings or carved-out niches. I made plaster casts, and transparent resin models, exploring the egg's function as a container. The comfortable, embracing curves suggest innumerable adaptations, some practical (furniture, for instance), and some totally fanciful. The egg shape is so welcoming and complete that once you let it inhabit your imagination, it will never leave.

Hollow shells, full shells. Think about them: Face up, they wait to serve as receptacles, for rain, for dust, for anything that happens to drop in. They are vulnerable and easily destroyed. But they can also be strengthened, and used to carry liquids and solids. To store things. To serve as scoops, ladles, moulds, boats. Face down, they become shelters, caves, protection from the elements. Or helmets, masks, hats.

Filled with solid matter, polished, the shells become monuments, sculptures, impervious to time and change. They might be rocks, or man-made structures of no apparent purpose except to reflect sunlight in different ways at different hours of the day. Are they ancient astronomical observatories? Or tombs containing the sealed mementoes of past civilizations?

Figure 86   Staged eggs, with mirror-foil

Figure 87   Project for an environment

Figure 88

Figure 89   Arrangement of plaster-filled eggshells

Cracked eggshells initiate a new train of thought: *ordered*, contrasted with *random* breakage. Look at the logical jigsaw pattern made by carefully flattening an eggshell without pulling it apart. Compare it to the random scattering of eggshell fragments. Both versions were once a complete shape, an eggshape. Prints, collages of torn or cut paper, line drawings, could serve as means of penetrating the implications and ramifications of this theme. And there is nothing to prevent us from pursuing it through the medium of *words*: we can construct an edifice of words, and break it up in random or in orderly fashion. And if we are sufficiently persistent, we will eventually run into the scientists' and the philosophers' questions and observations concerning order and randomness. In truly creative seeing, there is nothing which is unrelated to the subject at hand— because there is no subject which is not related to every other subject under the sun. But because we are unable to grasp this 'everything' in one glance, we focus on the egg. On the cracked eggshell. On the hollow space between two hands. On the peaks of the skin of a pineapple. On waves in water. On water. On our own reflection. . . . Creative education (which is primarily self-education) is, I think, a process of seeing the links between random fragments. While creation is a matter of making an entirely new pattern out of them.

Figure 90   Flattened eggshell

Figure 91   Scattered eggshell

Appendix

Natural Forms as Design Units

The following pictures of two other subjects, the cabbage and the onion, serve as examples of natural forms which can themselves be used as design modules.

The 'monolith' (Fig. 92) was formed by carefully cutting a rectangular section out of a cabbage. A close-up detail from it (Fig. 93) merits special attention, if you compare it to the wave patterns in Figs. 12, 13, 18. The loose cabbage cuttings (Fig. 94) have a fantasy-prodding quality, reminiscent of the flowing ink-on-water shapes (p. 29).

Cabbage parts can be used as stencils, they can be relief-printed, they can be cast in plaster, etc. They can be used to construct models, supporting fragile sections with wire, toothpicks or pins; more permanent constructions can be worked out from these maquettes.

The onion is perhaps the most varied design unit of all, a complete lesson in itself. If you slice it in half, either lengthways or across, and gently push out the separate sections, you have a display of perfectly related geometric forms, which can be re-combined in different ways, sliced into further sections, without ever losing their unity.

You can consider the onion as a set of bowls, stacked one inside the other. As thin rings piled up into a spherical shape. As boat-like shells wrapped round a core. Or as a compact package of thin skins, held together with a flexible glue.

Other natural forms which can be used include: Celery, artichoke, cauliflower, peppers, garlic, corn-cobs, various kinds of stems and leaves, chestnuts, pine-cones, innumerable flowers; the skeletons of leaves, of fish, etc. It is not a question of 'things you can make' out of such forms, but of examining and extracting their structural components as an aid to the study of design.

Figures 92–94   Cabbage parts

Figure 95 . Onion parts

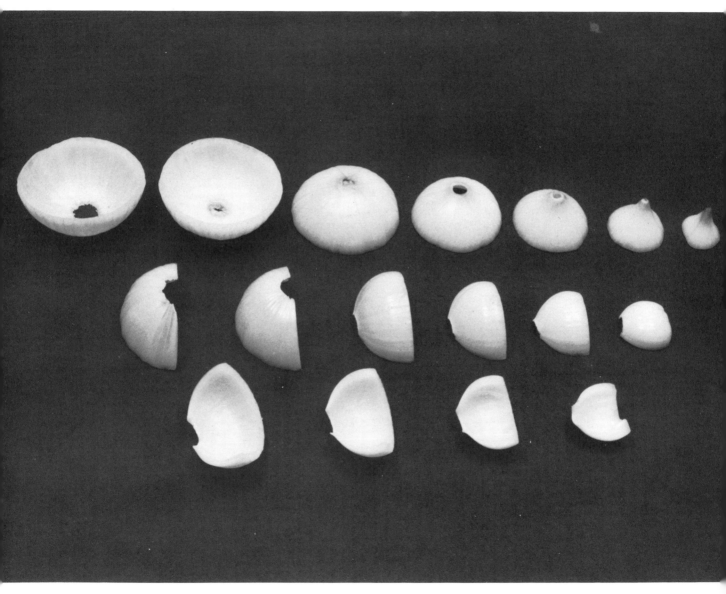

Figure 96   Onion cut in half

Visual Research

Students' Work

The staying-with-a-subject theme could be illustrated with enough examples from the work of past and present artists to produce an encyclopedia. But since my purpose has been to give a practical demonstration of the process itself while it takes place, I could only do this by using myself as guinea-pig. This does not mean that I am unaware of the fact that experiments along the lines of those which I have described are at this moment being carried out in many art schools and art departments, with extremely interesting and far-reaching results. It is impossible for me to know about them all, but those instances I have come in contact with reinforce my conviction that the area generally known as Visual Research, or simply VR, acts as a catalyst to the student, summoning to attention all of his or her creative resources.

My idea of an utopian art school would be an elaboration and extension of existing VR departments, in which natural forms would occupy a place of even greater importance than they do at present—in fact, it would consist of an environment specially designed to bring students and natural forms into close relationship, new relationships which they would not ordinarily experience.

An example of a particularly active and effective Visual Research department is the one at Hornsey College of Art in London. Given the opportunity to include illustrations of these students' work, but having a very limited space available in this book, I preferred to show only a handful of examples rather than crowd a few pages with postage stamp-size pictures. I selected those whose subjects coincided with or were related to mine. With extremely up-to-date and well-equipped work-shops at hand, a student's ideas can go through transformations into almost every conceivable medium. The following examples are only a small selection from a large body of work which the students produced around their chosen themes. The statements are by the students themselves.

Julia Barefoot (Hornsey College of Art. Second year, Dip.A.D., 3-Dimensional Design).

Shell studies: I was interested in the rhythmic twisting movement in the shell—the way the lines twisted round the form in an organic spiral, and in the undulating lines within the segments themselves. I was fascinated by the way the movements were gentle and light but also powerful and very structural. I concentrated on looking at one segment and began to visualize it as something much larger, perhaps even on an architectural scale. And I tried to create in three dimensions an assymetrical structure made up of a series of planes which suggested the twisting movement and also new undulating surfaces. I tried to capture something of the way the lines seemed to float in space. This later led towards ideas about furniture—perhaps most directly for furnishing textiles and lighting. But also I think it has been of great importance indirectly in helping me arrive at other shapes in other fields of furniture design.'

Figure 97   Julia Barefoot. Shell drawing

Figure 98   left   Julia Barefoot. Shell studies

79

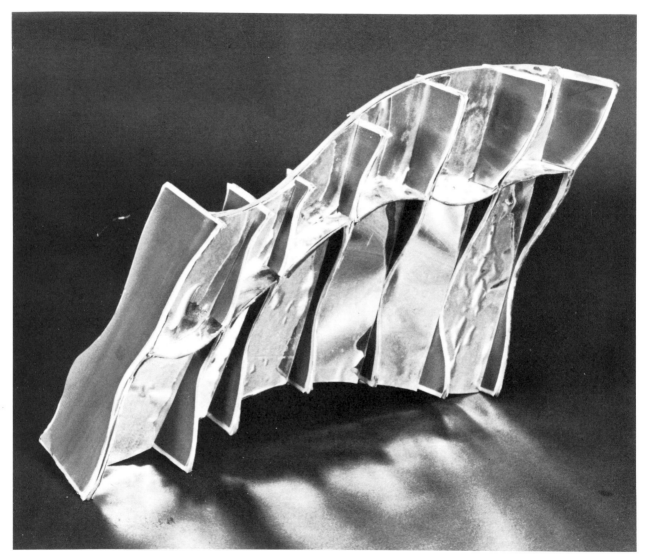

Figure 99   Julia Barefoot 3-dimensional
shell study

Figures 100   Keith Booth. Sketches of water movement

Keith Booth (*Hornsey College of Art. Second year, College Diploma, Ceramics*).

Water studies: 'The main point that I was trying to capture was not only the surface movement of water, but particularly the movement of water as a solid mass. And to try to reproduce this in two-dimensional media. Most of the original rough sketches were done very quickly to try to obtain this fluid movement. When I reached a stage where I thought I had achieved a method of presenting the movement, I started to try and find as many other ways as possible of using this method in order to achieve a design as opposed to a sketch.'

81

Figure 101 top left Keith Booth.
Water-movement study. Wire

Figure 102 right Keith Booth.
Water-movement study. Nails

Figure 103 lower left Keith Booth.
Water studies

Helen Pieri (Hornsey College of Art. Second Year, Dip.A.D., Graphic Design).

Project on Liquids: 'I intended to explore the nature of liquids intermixing and reacting. Soap was used to hold together oil, coloured inks and water, preserving these in static formation to enable me to make a series of drawings. As a further development, marbling inks were used but I found that these were less successful than my later use of black oil-based ink and water —the monochromatic image being better defined. The patterns formed in the water were selected for their rhythmic qualities and recorded by offsetting on paper quickly as they changed.

Figures 104 and 105   Helen Pieri.
3-dimensional studies of liquid motion

Areas were selected by intercutting. Appropriate rhythmic textures were used to create illusions of pouring, flowing and drinking. Using photography, I attempted to push the illusions to the point of credibility and found that this, in fact, strengthened the illusion. In the next stage, selected areas were collaged and photographed on high-contrast film, simplifying and resolving the inherent rhythms. A three-dimensional equivalent wood structure was created as a development of the linear rhythms contained in the recorded images; colour being manipulated to clarify the harmonious linear relationships.'

Edna Kurz (*Hornsey College of Art. Second Year, Dip.A.D., Graphic Design*).

Visual Research Project: 'I started out by wondering if a piece of furniture could be made which was at once firm and soft. I first of all thought about various cushions. It then occurred to me that the human hand was a shape which could allow for the change from soft formlessness to a supporting structure. The idea stood or fell—as the chair stood or fell—on whether the soft material of its construction could simply, by the weight of a sitting body, be transferred into a fairly rigid structure. If the chair is not sat in, the fingers are unable to keep their equilibrium. But once weight is placed in the seat the polystyrene is forced up the fingers and they stand rigidly. Therefore, it becomes solid only when it needs to be solid. If I had simply taken the human hand as a model, obviously the fingers would be too long and the shape of the palm and its back would be inadequate as a structural base. The chair's ability to change is, therefore, a matter of its proportions and these were reached by experiment. As a chair, it is designed for use and for different sorts of use so the material had to be strong and the seams very carefully designed. I wanted people to take liberties with the chair, to pull it about, to lie on it, to sit on the thumb or with the fingers folded, even to throw it at each other. The 'feeling' about it that I liked was to do with its malleability, its friendly firmness when wanted, its capaciousness and lightness compared with its size. A jolly and helping hand.'

Figure 106   Edna Kurz. Hand-chair

Links and References

It became evident to me during the course of preparing this book that every idea which arises out of close communion with a subject is like one filament in a giant spider-web. As soon as your mind fastens upon it, the whole web starts vibrating and you suddenly just 'happen' to come across extraordinary coincidences: a book, a picture, a sentence from an article, an object in a shop-window, a person who happens to be a professional in the very field you want to ask questions about. Sometimes, the profusion of unexpected links can be overwhelming and frustrating. You feel that you will never be able to cope with it all. My solution is to take from my ever-growing stockpile of reference material only those items which I can use directly: that is, those which provoke questions or ideas which I can pursue with my own methods, in my own 'language'.

This may be a very utilitarian view of learning, but it is one which I an advocating unashamedly. I hope that my book will be considered with the same 'what's in it for *me*?' attitude with which I have regarded the books I consulted in my search.

I make no pretence of scientific thoroughness. Some of the highly complex areas which these works deal with should be investigated in many more volumes than this bibliography mentions. I have left out a great deal. My enthusiasm for a subject has often led me to rush home with a weighty and expensive tome, opened at random on an illuminating paragraph, only to find the rest of the admirable treatise totally incomprehensible. I console myself that the one 'Open Sesame' paragraph was intended for *me* to use. Do I mean the artist's use of everything around him as material for his work? Yes, if you wish. But, as the practice of awareness can lead to the creation of works of art, so, too, does the practice of art sometimes lead to pure awareness. And in the domain of awareness, the experts, the successful, are those for whom life is made more intense, more constantly surprising, by their own awareness of it.

Water

1 *What is Light?* A. C. S. van Heel and C. H. F. Velzel, World University Library, London 1968, pp. 63–68, 'Interference'. Explaining, with a water-wave model, how two or more wave systems interact, creating ripple patterns.

2   *Light and Vision*, Conrad G. Mueller, Mae Rudolph and the Editors of TIME-LIFE BOOKS, Time-Life Books Pocket Edition 1969, pp. 38–39, Thomas Young experiment on how waves in water behave, to illustrate light-waves. P. 40, laboratory photograph of water ripples hitting a barrier.

3   *An Introduction to the Theory of Diffraction*, C. J. Ball, The Commonwealth and International Library, Pergamon Press, Oxford, New York, Toronto 1971, p. 50, diagram, 'Fresnel zones'.

4   *Mathematics in Art*, Michael Holt, Studio Vista, London; Van Nostrand Reinhold Co. New York 1971, p. 38, the Fraser Spiral (from E. H. Gombrich's *Art and Illusion*).

5   *Leonardo da Vinci* (selections from the notebooks). Edited with commentaries by Irma A. Richter, Oxford University Press, London 1966, pp. 23–26, 'Of Waves': *'The wave is the recoil of the stroke and it will be greater or less in proportion as the stroke is greater or less. A wave is never alone but is mingled with as many other waves as there are inequalities on the banks where the wave is produced. . . .'*; pp. 37–38, 'Water and Air'. *'The movement of water within water proceeds like that of air within air.' 'Just as the stone thrown into water becomes the centre and cause of various circles, and the sound made in the air spreads out in circles, so every body placed within the luminous air spreads itself out in circles and fills the surrounding parts with an infinite number of images of itself, and appears all in all and all in each part.'*

6   *Physics Made Simple*, Ira M. Freeman, Made Simple Books, W. H. Allen, London 1967, pp. 105–123, 'The Nature of Sound, Acoustics'. Fig. 65: Ripple tray. Fig. 68: Stationary wave patterns on vibrating rope. Fig. 73: Wave forms of various sources.

7   *Sound* (HOW & WHY Wonder Books Series), Martin L. Keen and George J. Zaffo, Transworld Publishers, London; Wonder Books Inc., New York 1962. Intended for children, but very useful for any age, especially if you like to *see* things demonstrated rather than explained in theory only.

8   *Light and Colour* (HOW & WHY Wonder Book Series), Harold Joseph Highland and George J. Zaffo, Transworld

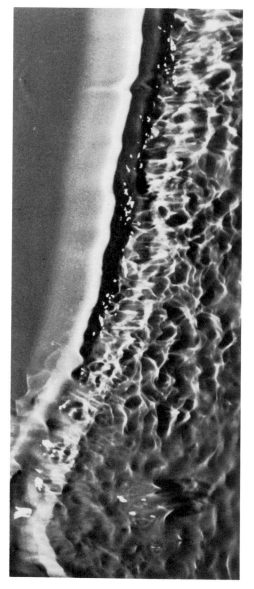

Publishers, London; Wonder Books Inc., New York 1963, pp. 34–35, wave frequency: diagram of parts of a wave.

9 *The Waves—The Nature of Sea Motion*, George M. Hidy, Van Nostrand Reinhold Co., New York 1971, pp. 120–121, 'The Structure of Turbulence'.

10 *Sleep*, Ian Oswald, Pelican Original, Penguin Books, Harmondsworth, Middlesex; Baltimore, Maryland, 1966, p. 101, Fig. 7: Diagram of two kinds of sleep, showing various wave forms or EEG (electroencephalogram) records.

11 *Aspects of Form*, ed. by Lancelot Law Whyte, Lund Humphries, London 1968, pp. 179–195: 'Activity Patterns in the Human Brain' by W. Grey Walter. See especially the discussion of alpha rhythms, pp. 182–186, which led me to these conjectures:

The effort of paying attention has generally been found to block or arrest alpha activity in most people (alpha waves have been called the 'waves of inattention'). However, alpha activity (seen as very fine ripples on EEG records) has been found to correlate with habits of thought and imagination. It occurred to me that a criss-crossing of the fine alpha-ripples of relaxed receptivity with the sharply zigzagging waves of concentrated attention, might—if you could see it actually happening—look like the interference patterns observed in light-diffraction. And that these orderly wave patterns might be that state of mind which we call 'creative'. Oddly enough, an alternation between intense attention and a 'mindless' receptivity is precisely the advice given in Yoga teachings:

12 *Yoga*, Ernest Wood, Pelican, Penguin Books, Harmondsworth, Middlesex; Baltimore, Maryland, 1959, p. 237: *'Concentration is the holding of the mind to one object of attention, be it simple or complex, small or large, concrete or abstract. Practice is according to ability—in most cases simple, small and concrete in the beginning.*
Meditation is full exercise of thought about that object. Contemplation takes place when the thought-supply is exhausted, and one continues attentively looking, without desire or thought or wish or will, until intuition or insight or illumination comes.

These three are practised as one act, called 'sanyama', which leads to the reduction of the habit of mind-spreading and increase of the power of one-pointedness.' (Copyright Ernest Wood 1959.)

13   *The Compleat Astrologer*, Derek and Julia Parker, Mitchell Beazley Ltd., London 1971, pp. 48, 49: Diagrams. Activity cycles (wave forms) in human body. pp. 52–53: Electromagnetic spectrum. Chart of universal activity scale, in wavelengths and cycles.

14   *Art and Visual Perception*, Rudolf Arnheim, Faber and Faber, London 1967, pp. 247–248: 'A Brain Model', Fig. 193. The author uses the Chinese abacus as a means of visualizing the cortex as a three-dimensional field, in which the stimuli received from the retinas would be the 'beads'. They can slide freely along the parallel wires, in an infinite number of planes. I like this illustration, since it accords with my interpretations of waves as 'bumps' in a set of parallel lines.

15   *Scientific American*, September 1968 issue on LIGHT. Scientific American Inc., 415 Madison Ave., New York, N.Y. 10017. This whole issue is of absorbing interest and relevance. See particularly pp. 204–214: 'The Processes of Vision' by Ulric Neisser.

16   *Eye and Brain*, R. L. Gregory, World University Library, Weidenfeld and Nicolson, London 1966, pp. 7–12: examples of how things can be seen as objects or patterns; ambiguous figures.
Chapter 12: 'Seeing and believing'. Relevant to the idea that we 'fill in the blanks' between patterns in space, to create recognizable objects.

17   *On Growth and Form*, D'Arcy Thompson, Cambridge University Press, London and New York 1961, This book is a gold-mine of information, inspiration and illustrations relevant to our themes. It is impossible to point out every item of specific interest without quoting nearly the whole book. Suffice to say that in its pages you can find explanations which are not final but allow you many choices and open up vast areas for imaginative investigation.

18 *Sensitive Chaos: the creation of flowing forms in water and air*, Theodor Schwenk, Rudolf Steiner Press, London 1965. A work of such usefulness to the water-theme, and to the approach which I have been discussing, that I regret having discovered it only at the end of my experiments for this book. The illustrations, both diagrams and photographs, are tremendously stimulating. See especially pp. 24–39 (trains of vortices); pp. 46–54 (underwater streams of liquid flowing into still water); and the diagrams on pp. 37–43, showing resemblances between waves in water, the human embryo, the chrysalis of a butterfly, mountain ranges, etc., through their common process of the *hollowing out* of inner spaces, leading to the vortex-form.

19 *Water*, Luna B. Leopold, Kenneth S. Davis and the Editors of TIME-LIFE BOOKS, Time-Life Books Pocket Edition 1970.

20 *Water, The Mirror of Science*, Kenneth S. Davis and John Arthur Day, Heinemann Educational 1964.

21 *Water, Miracle of Nature*, Thomson King, Collier-Macmillan 1961.

22 *Soap Bubbles and the Forces that Mould Them*, C. V. Boys, Dover, New York 1959.

23 *Crystals and Light: An Introduction to Optical Crystallography*, Elizabeth A. Wood, Van Nostrand Momentum Books, Van Nostrand Co., London and New York 1964. This very helpful paperback gives you a strip of polarizing film and a number of experiments on how to use it, in which the observation of ice-crystals is included (p. 111).

24 *Waves of the Sea and other Water Waves*, V. Cornish, London 1910 (50 illustrations); *Waves of Sand and Snow, and the Eddies which make them*, V. Cornish, London 1914 (80 illustrations); *Ocean Waves and kindred Geophysical Phenomena*, V. Cornish, London 1934.

25 *A Study of Splashes*, A. M. Worthington, London 1908. (200 photographs of splashes.)

Pineapple

26 *On Growth and Form*, D'Arcy Thompson (see No. 17 of this list), pp. 88–102: 'The Forms of Tissues, or Cell-Aggregates'; pp. 103–119: 'Hexagonal Symmetry'; pp. 119–124: 'The Partitioning of Space'. The mechanical principle behind the hexagonal pattern so often found in nature seems to be that this pattern is the necessary result of equal pressures: the more forces there are acting in conjunction and opposing each other (such as the vibrations against the sides of the water-filled basin, which produced the wave-patterns resembling a pineapple's skin, a wasp's nest, etc.), the more mechanical resistance is produced, and the more regular and perfect the pattern.

27 *Aspects of Form* (see No. 11 of this list), p. 57–76: 'Form in Plants,' by F. G. Gregory; p. 62: *'Four characteristics of light exert direct effect upon the form of plants: intensity, quality, duration, and direction.'* Consider this statement in terms of waves in water, as well as form in plants: are they not the same characteristics—intensity, quality, duration and direction—which, if translated into vibrations, would shape the patterns of ripples and waves?; p. 74: The origin of the symmetry in plants.

28 *Design as Art*, Bruno Munari, A Pelican Original, Penguin Books Ltd., Harmondsworth, Middlesex 1971, pp. 156–214: 'Research Design'. Especially 'Growth and Explosion', pp. 158–162. A brilliant little book, which should be a designer's bible. Concise, illuminating and humorous.

29 *Order in Space*, Keith Critchlow, Thames and Hudson, London 1969 (a design source book). To be read, looked at and used slowly, with great concentration. Then play with it. P. 84: Links proportional value systems and geometric patterns with symbolic, religious and occult traditions, e.g. hexagon as Star of David, *'the sixfold symbol of creation and perfection expressed in divine power, majesty, wisdom, love, mercy and justice'* (cit. from *Signs & Symbols in Christian Art*, George Ferguson, Oxford University Press, 1961). The hexagon and six-pointed star in Oriental symbolism. The *I Ching*, or Book of Changes, in which the hexagram plays a vital part, etc.

30 *Mathematics in Art* (see No. 4 of this list), Michael Holt. Very useful and thought-provoking.

31 *The Curves of Life*, T. Cook, London 1914 (spirals in nature and art based on manuscripts of Leonardo da Vinci).

32 *Symmetry*, Hermann Weyl, Princeton University Press, 1952.

33 *The Plant Kingdom*, Harold C. Bold, Foundations of Modern Biology Series, Prentice-Hall Inc., New Jersey; Prentice-Hall International, London 1970, pp. 156–157: on the pineapple.

34 *The Natural Philosophy of Plant Form*, Agnes Arber, Oxford 1950. (A study of plant morphology.)

35 *Design: A Search for Essentials*, E. A. Hurwitz, International Textbooks, New York 1964. Described in the Tiranti Bookshop catalogue for 1967 as: *'Man's desire to create, the creative process, and natural beauty and form around us'*. (Tiranti Art Bookshop, 72 Charlotte St., London W.1.)

36 *Morphanalysis*, Graham Rabey, Wellcome Research Fellow, Middlesex Hospital, London; Mount Vernon Hospital, Northwood 1968. Available from H. K. Lewis & Co. Ltd., 136 Gower St., London WC1E 6BS. A very interesting and original study of morphology, with many aspects relevant to our research.

37 *Creating a Role*, Constantin Stanislavski, NEL Mentor Edition, The New English Library, London 1968. I am including this book because, although it was intended for actors, it is also of vital interest to the artist, and to anyone involved in the creative process. I don't know whether Stanislavski's work is as well-known and appreciated among art-students as it is in the field of drama, but it certainly merits re-examining from the visual artist's point of view. Stanislavski's *psychotechnique*, intended to teach the actor to establish 'a true inner creative state while on the stage', ought to be studied and practised in conjunction with the kind of experiments which I have suggested.

The Hand

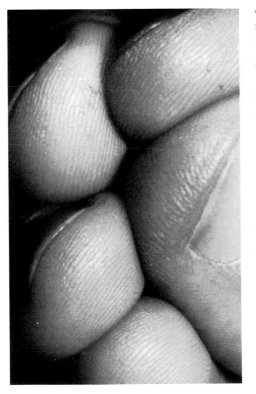

38 *The Body*, Alan E. Nourse and the Editors of TIME-LIFE BOOKS, Time-Life Books Pocket Edition 1969, pp. 150–151: touch-sensitivity of the hand illustrated; pp. 24–25; fingerprint patterns.

39 *Anatomical Atlas*, Maud Jepson, John Murray, London 1970, p. 7: bones of the hands.

40 *The Human Hand*, Charlotte Wolff, London 1944; *Psychology of Gesture*, Charlotte Wolff, Methuen, London 1945.

41 *Mudras, the Ritual Hand Poses of the Buddha Priests and Shiva Priests of Bali*, T. De Kleen, London 1924. (With 60 drawings of hand-gesture language.)

42 *Play with Light and Shadow* (art and techniques of shadow theatre), Herta Schönewolf, Studio Vista, London; Reinhold Book Corporation, New York 1968.

43 *Creative Drawing, Point and Line*, Ernst Rottger and Dieter Klante, B. T. Batsford Ltd., London 1969, pp. 82–83: Two-handed line drawing (see also pp. 35–49, in relation to WAVES).

44 *Grafilm*, an approach to a new medium. J. Bryne-Daniel, Studio Vista, London; Van Nostrand Reinhold Co., New York 1970. Describes techniques and suggests projects for working directly on film stock, to make 'Grafilms'. Opens up exciting possibilities for anyone interested in putting their graphic ideas into motion.

45 *Scientific American*, September 1968 issue. Scientific American Inc., New York, pp. 218–224: 'Mathematical Games', counting systems and the relationship between numbers and the real world, by Martin Gardner. Useful article and illustrations showing number systems with finger-positions.

46 *Mathematical Puzzles and Diversions*, Martin Gardner, Pelican, Harmondsworth, Middlesex.

47 *The Elements of Dynamic Symmetry*, J. Hambridge, Dover, New York.

48 *Mathematics in Art*, Michael Holt (see No. 4 of this list), pp. 72–81; 'Ambidextrous Art.'

49 *The Graphic Work of M. C. Escher*, Oldbourne, London 1967

50 *The Ambidextrous Universe: Left, Right, and the Fall of Parity*, Martin Gardner, Pelican, Harmondsworth, Middlesex 1964. Fascinating and mind-bending book. Absolutely required reading.

51 *The History of Magic*, Kurt Seligmann, Pantheon Books, New York 1948, pp. 397–409: Chiromancy. Good illustrations.

Eggs

I have not found any books specifically related to the egg-form. Works about form (aesthetics, etc.) in general are too varied and numerous to attempt listing here. I will cite only:

52 *The Act of Creation*, Arthur Koestler, Pan Books Ltd. (paperback), London 1970. This book *'proposes a theory of the act of creation—of the conscious and unconscious processes underlying scientific discovery, artistic originality, and comic inspiration. It endeavours to show that all creative activities have a basic pattern in common, and to outline that pattern.'* (quote from the Preface to the original edition). I don't think I have ever come across another book which is so charged with the power to set one's mind racing up the slopes and diving into the oceans of that little-known continent we call creativity. It positively crackles with the author's own energy, and that of all the artists, scientists, authors, poets, from whose lives and works he selects appropriate examples to illustrate his theme. It is a book to be carried around and read a little at a time, as nearly every page provokes one to ask questions, to propose answers, and to pursue in one's own way the ideas which Koestler initiates.

Techniques

Of relevance to methods mentioned in this book:

Plaster Casting for the Student Sculptor, Victor H. Wager, Scopas Handbook, Alec Tiranti, London 1970.

New Materials in Sculpture, H. M. Percy, Alec Tiranti, London 1965.

Plastics as an Art Form, Thelma R. Newman, Pitman, London 1965; Chilton, Philadelphia and New York, 1964.

Printmaking: a medium for basic design, Peter Weaver, Studio Vista, London; Reinhold Book Corp., New York, 1968.

Creative Casting: Jewellery, Silverware, Sculpture, S. Choates,

Modern Glass, Geoffrey Beard, Studio Vista, London 1968.

Three Methods of Marbling, J. S. Hewitt-Bates and J. Halliday, Dryad Leaflet No. 74, The Dryad Press, Northgates, Leicester.

Animated Film Making, Anthony Kinsey, Studio Vista, London 1970.

Plastics for Artists and Craftsmen, Harry B. Hollander, Watson-Guptill Publications, New York, 1972.

Sculpture in Plastics, Nicholas Roukes, Watson-Guptill Publications, New York, 1970.

Abstraction in Art and Nature, Nathan Cabot Hale, Watson-Guptill Publications, New York, 1972.

Materials

Re-meltable rubber (for making flexible moulds): same address as above, ALLCRAFT. A useful catalogue is available from this firm, including details of enamelling equipment, etc.

General materials and equipment for sculpture, etc.: Tiranti, 72 Charlotte Street, London W1P 2AJ.

An inexpensive but very adequate microscope for our purposes is the: SCIENTIST X20 MICROSCOPE available from: C. E. Offord, Hurst Green, Etchingham, Sussex, England.

Clear resin (for casting, embedding, etc.): *Crystal Cast* from ALLCRAFT, 61b High Street, Watford WD1 2DJ, Herts.

Other resin suppliers
Bondaglass Limited, 158–164 Ravenscroft Road, Beckenham, Kent

Dow Corning Limited, Educational suppliers: Hopkin and Williams, Ducie Street, Manchester 1

Isopon Interchemicals, Industrial Estate, Maylands Avenue, Hemel Hempstead, Herts

Suppliers in the USA

Resins
Resin Coatings Corporation, 14940 N.W. 25 Court Opa Locka, Florida 33054

Polyproducts Corporation, Order Department, Room 25, 13810 Nelson Ave., Detroit, Michigan 48227

Sculpture supplies (mail-order catalogs available)
Amaco Products, (American Art Clay Company, Inc.), 4717 West 16th Street, Indianapolis, Indiana 46222

Sculpture Associates, 114 East 25th Street, New York, N.Y. 10010

Sculpture House, 38 East 30th Street, New York, N.Y. 10016

General art supplies (mail-order catalogs available)
A. I. Friedman Inc., 25 West 45th Street, New York, N.Y. 10036

Arthur Brown & Bro. Inc., 2 West 46th Street, New York, N.Y. 10036